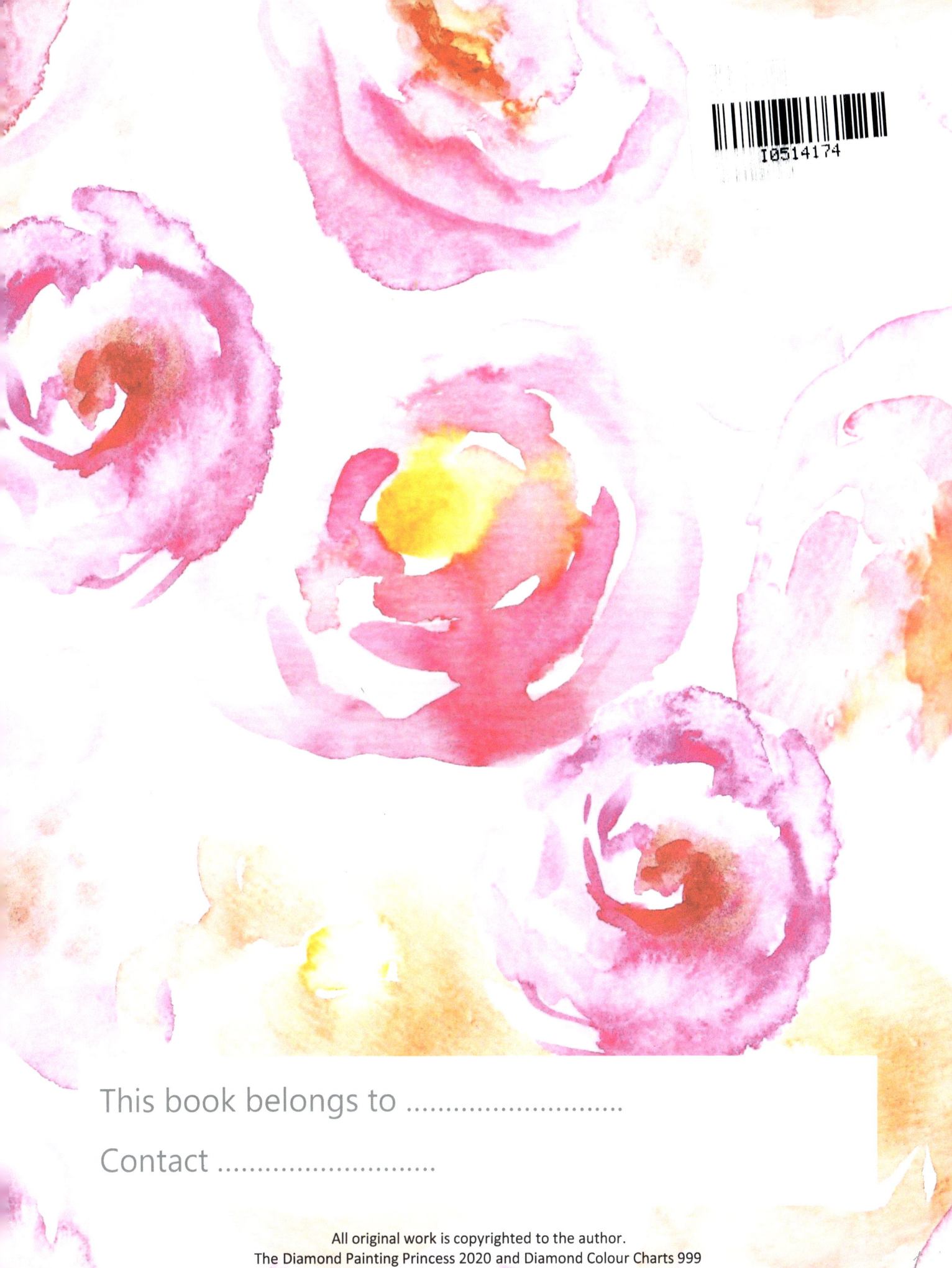

This book belongs to ....

Contact ....

All original work is copyrighted to the author.
The Diamond Painting Princess 2020 and Diamond Colour Charts 999

Contents

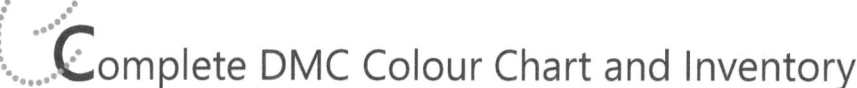

Complete DMC Colour Chart and Inventory   3 - 9

This complete colour chart details the DMC number along with a swatch for each diamond colour.
There are four columns labelled "SQ", "RND", "AB SQ" and "AB RND". These columns allow you to keep an inventory of any spare drills you have by sticking them in and using the colour chart as a quick 'look up' guide. This is a quick way to see what colour drills are available in your stock.

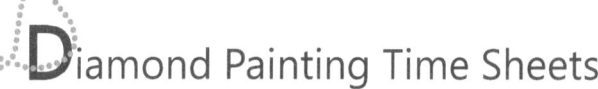

Diamond Painting Time Sheets   10 - 11

Use these pages to keep a track of the time spent your projects.

Diamond Painting Log Book   12 - 37

Keep track of your Diamond painting projects. Use these log book pages to keep track of the diamond paintings you are currently working on or ones that you have completed in the past.

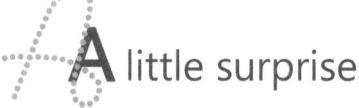

A little surprise!   39

DMC COLOUR CHART
Ecru - 310

No.	Name	Colour	SQ	RND	AB SQ	AB RND	No.	Name	Colour	SQ	RND	AB SQ	AB RND
Ecru	Ecru/off-white						34	Fuchsia - DK					
Blanc	White						35	Fuchsia - VY DK					
White	White						150	Red - BRIGHT					
1	White Tin						151	Pink					
2	Tin						152	Tawny - DK					
3	Tin - MED						153	Lilac					
4	Tin - DK						154	Red - VY DK					
5	Driftwood - LT						155	Forget-me-not Blue					
6	Driftwood - MED LT						156	Blue - MED					
7	Driftwood						157	Blue - LT					
8	Driftwood - DK						158	Blue - DK					
9	Cocoa - VY DK						159	Petrol Blue - LT					
10	Tender Green - VY LT						160	Petrol Blue - MED					
11	Tender Green - LT						161	Petrol Blue - DK					
12	Tender Green						162	Baby Blue - LT					
13	Nile Green - MED LT						163	Green					
14	Apple Green - PALE						164	Green - LT					
15	Apple Green						165	Green - BRIGHT					
16	Chartreuse - LT						166	Lime Green					
17	Yellow Plum - LT						167	Khaki Brown					
18	Yellow Plum						168	Silver Gray					
19	Autumn Gold - MED LT						169	Pewter Gray					
20	Shrimp						208	Lavender - VY DK					
21	Alizarian - LT						209	Lavender - DK					
22	Alizarian						210	Lavender - MED					
23	Apple Blossom						211	Lavender - LT					
24	White Lavender						221	Shell Pink - VY DK					
25	Lavender - ULTRA LT						223	Shell Pink - LT					
26	Lavender - PALE						224	Shell Pink - VY LT					
27	White Violet						225	Shell Pink - ULT VY LT					
28	Eggplant - MED LT						300	Mahogany - VY DK					
29	Eggplant						301	Mahogany - MED					
30	Blueberry - MED LT						304	Red - MED					
31	Blueberry						307	Lemon					
32	Blueberry - DK						309	Rose - DK					
33	Fuchsia						310	Black					

311 - 554

No.	Name	Colour	SQ	RND	AB SQ	AB RND	No.	Name	Colour	SQ	RND	AB SQ	AB RND
311	Blue - MED						415	Pearl Gray					
312	Baby Blue - VY DK						420	Hazelnut Brown - DK					
315	Antique Mauve - MED DK						422	Hazelnut Brown - LT					
316	Antique Mauve - MED						433	Brown - MED					
317	Pewter Gray						434	Brown - LT					
318	Steel Gray - LT						435	Brown - VY LT					
319	Pistachio Green - VY DK						436	Tan					
320	Pistachio Green - MED						437	Tan - LT					
321	Red						444	Lemon - DK					
322	Baby Blue						445	Lemon - LT					
326	Rose - VY DK						451	Shell Gray - DK					
327	Violet						452	Shell Gray - MED					
333	Blue Violet - VY DK						453	Shell Gray - LT					
334	Baby Blue - MED						469	Avocado Green					
335	Rose						470	Avocado Green - LT					
336	Blue						471	Avocado Green - VY LT					
340	Blue Violet - MED						472	Avocado Green - ULT LT					
341	Blue Violet - LT						498	Red - DK					
347	Salmon - VY DK						500	Blue Green - VY DK					
349	Coral - DK						501	Blue Green - DK					
350	Coral - MED						502	Blue Green					
351	Coral						503	Blue Green - MED					
352	Coral - LT						504	Blue Green - VY LT					
353	Peach						505	Grass Green - DK					
355	Terra Cotta - DK						517	Wedgewood - DK					
356	Terra Cotta - MED						518	Wedgewood - LT					
367	Pistachio Green - DK						519	Sky Blue					
368	Pistachio Green - LT						520	Fern Green - DK					
369	Pistachio Green - VY LT						522	Fern Green					
370	Mustard - MED						523	Fern Green - LT					
371	Mustard						524	Fern Green - VY LT					
372	Mustard - LT						535	Ash Gray - VY LT					
400	Mahogany - DK						543	Beige Brown - ULT VY LT					
402	Mahogany - VY LT						550	Violet - VY DK					
407	Desert Sand - DK						552	Violet - MED					
413	Pewter Gray - DK						553	Violet					
414	Steel Gray - DK						554	Violet - LT					

561 - 779

No.	Name	Colour	SQ	RND	AB SQ	AB RND	No.	Name	Colour	SQ	RND	AB SQ	AB RND
561	Jade - VY DK						704	Chartreuse - BRIGHT					
562	Jade - MED						712	Cream					
563	Jade - LT						718	Plum					
564	Jade - VY LT						720	Orange Spice - DK					
580	Moss Green - DK						721	Orange Spice - MED					
581	Moss Green						722	Orange Spice - LT					
597	Turquoise						725	Topaz					
598	Turquoise - LT						726	Topaz - LT					
600	Cranberry - VY DK						727	Topaz - VY LT					
601	Cranberry - DK						728	Golden Yellow					
602	Cranberry - MED						729	Old Gold - MED					
603	Cranberry						730	Olive Green - VY DK					
604	Cranberry - LT						731	Olive Green - DK					
605	Cranberry - VY LT						732	Olive Green					
606	Orange-red - BRIGHT						733	Olive Green - MED					
608	Orange - BRIGHT						734	Olive Green - LT					
610	Drab Brown - DK						738	Tan - VY LT					
611	Drab Brown						739	Tan - ULT VY LT					
612	Drab Brown - LT						740	Tangerine					
613	Drab Brown - VY LT						741	Tangerine - MED					
632	Desert Sand - ULT VY DK						742	Tangerine - LT					
640	Beige Gray - VY DK						743	Yellow - MED					
642	Beige Gray - DK						744	Yellow - PALE					
644	Beige Gray - MED						745	Yellow - LT PALE					
645	Beaver Gray - VY DK						746	Off White					
646	Beaver Gray - DK						747	Sky Blue - VY LT					
647	Beaver Gray - MED						754	Peach - LT					
648	Beaver Gray - LT						758	Terra Cotta - VY LT					
666	Red - BRIGHT						760	Salmon					
676	Old Gold - LT						761	Salmon - LT					
677	Old Gold - VY LT						762	Pearl Gray - VY LT					
680	Old Gold - DK						772	Yellow Green - VY LT					
699	Green						775	Baby Blue - VY LT					
700	Green - BRIGHT						776	Pink - MED					
701	Green - LT						777	Red - DEEP					
702	Kelly Green						778	Antique Mauve - VY LT					
703	Chartreuse						779	Brown					

780 - 924

No.	Name	Colour	SQ	RND	AB SQ	AB RND	No.	Name	Colour	SQ	RND	AB SQ	AB RND
780	Topaz - ULT VY DK						833	Golden Olive - LT					
781	Topaz - VY DK						834	Golden Olive - VY LT					
782	Topaz - DK						838	Beige Brown - VY DK					
783	Topaz - MED						839	Beige Brown - DK					
791	Cornflower Blue - VY DK						840	Beige Brown - MED					
792	Cornflower Blue - DK						841	Beige Brown - LT					
793	Cornflower Blue - MED						842	Beige Brown - VY LT					
794	Cornflower Blue - LT						844	Beaver Gray - ULT DK					
796	Royal Blue - DK						868	Hazel Nut Brown					
797	Royal Blue						869	Hazelnut Brown - VY DK					
798	Delft Blue - DK						890	Pistachio Green - ULT DK					
799	Delft Blue - MED						891	Carnation - DK					
800	Delft Blue - PALE						892	Carnation - MED					
801	Coffee Brown - DK						893	Carnation - LT					
803	Blue - DEEP						894	Carnation - VY LT					
806	Peacock Blue - DK						895	Hunter Green - VY DK					
807	Peacock Blue						898	Coffee Brown - VY DK					
809	Delft Blue						899	Rose - MED					
813	Blue - LT						900	Burnt Orange - DK					
814	Garnet - DK						902	Garnet - VY DK					
815	Garnet - MED						904	Parrot Green - VY DK					
816	Garnet						905	Parrot Green - DK					
817	Coral Red - VY DK						906	Parrot Green - MED					
818	Baby Pink						907	Parrot Green - LT					
819	Baby Pink - LT						909	Emerald Green - VY DK					
820	Royal Blue - VY DK						910	Emerald Green - DK					
822	Beige Gray - LT						911	Emerald Green - MED					
823	Blue - DK						912	Emerald Green - LT					
824	Blue - VY DK						913	Nile Green - MED					
825	Blue - DK						915	Plum - DK					
826	Blue - MED						917	Plum - MED					
827	Blue - VY LT						918	Red Copper - DK					
828	Blue - ULT VY LT						919	Red Copper					
829	Golden Olive - VY DK						920	Copper - MED					
830	Golden Olive - DK						921	Copper					
831	Golden Olive - MED						922	Copper - LT					
832	Golden Olive						924	Gray Green - VY DK					

926 - 3345

No.	Name	Colour	SQ	RND	AB SQ	AB RND	No.	Name	Colour	SQ	RND	AB SQ	AB RND
926	Gray Green - MED						977	Golden Brown - LT					
927	Gray Green - LT						986	Forest Green - VY DK					
928	Gray Green - VY LT						987	Forest Green - DK					
930	Antique Blue - DK						988	Forest Green - MED					
931	Antique Blue - MED						989	Forest Green					
932	Antique Blue - LT						991	Aquamarine - DK					
934	Avocado Green - BLACK						992	Aquamarine - LT					
935	Avocado Green - DK						993	Aquamarine - VY LT					
936	Avocado Green - VY DK						995	Electric Blue - DK					
937	Avocado Green - MED						996	Electric Blue - MED					
938	Coffee Brown - ULT DK						3011	Khaki Green - DK					
939	Blue - VY DK						3012	Khaki Green - MED					
943	Aquamarine - MED						3013	Khaki Green - LT					
945	Tawny						3021	Brown Gray - VY DK					
946	Burnt Orange - MED						3022	Brown Gray - MED					
947	Burnt Orange						3023	Brown Gray - LT					
948	Peach - VY LT						3024	Brown Gray - VY LT					
950	Desert Sand - LT						3031	Mocha Brown - VY DK					
951	Tawny - LT						3032	Mocha Brown - MED					
954	Nile Green						3033	Mocha Brown - VY LT					
955	Nile Green - LT						3041	Antique Violet - MED					
956	Geranium						3042	Antique Violet - LT					
957	Geranium - PALE						3045	Yellow Beige - DK					
958	Seagreen - DK						3046	Yellow Beige - MED					
959	Seagreen - MED						3047	Yellow Beige - LT					
961	Dusty Rose - DK						3051	Green Gray - DK					
962	Dusty Rose - MED						3052	Green Gray - MED					
963	Dusty Rose - ULT VY LT						3053	Green Gray					
964	Seagreen - LT						3064	Desert Sand					
966	Baby Green - MED						3072	Beaver Gray - VY LT					
967	Peach - LT						3078	Golden Yellow - VY LT					
970	Pumpkin - LT						3325	Baby Blue - LT					
971	Pumpkin						3326	Rose - LT					
972	Canary - DEEP						3328	Salmon - DK					
973	Canary - BRIGHT						3340	Apricot - MED					
975	Golden Brown - DK						3341	Apricot					
976	Golden Brown - MED						3345	Hunter Green - DK					

3346 - 3818

No.	Name	Colour	SQ	RND	AB SQ	AB RND	No.	Name	Colour	SQ	RND	AB SQ	AB RND
3346	Hunter Green						3760	Wedgewood - MED					
3347	Yellow Green - MED						3761	Sky Blue - LT					
3348	Yellow Green - LT						3765	Peacock Blue - VY DK					
3350	Dusty Rose - ULT DK						3766	Peacock Blue - LT					
3354	Dusty Rose - LT						3768	Gray Green - DK					
3362	Pine Green - DK						3770	Tawny - VY LT					
3363	Pine Green - MED						3771	Peach - DK					
3364	Pine Green						3772	Desert Sand - VY DK					
3371	Black Brown						3773	Desert Sand - MED					
3607	Plum - LT						3774	Desert Sand - VY LT					
3608	Plum - VY LT						3776	Mahogany - LT					
3609	Plum - ULT LT						3777	Terra Cotta - VY DK					
3685	Mauve - VY DK						3778	Terra Cotta - LT					
3687	Mauve						3779	Terra Cotta - ULT VY LT					
3688	Mauve - MED						3781	Mocha Brown - DK					
3689	Mauve - LT						3782	Mocha Brown - LT					
3705	Melon - DK						3787	Brown Gray - DK					
3706	Melon - MED						3790	Beige Gray - ULT DK					
3708	Melon - LT						3799	Pewter Gray - VY DK					
3712	Salmon - MED						3801	Melon - VY DK					
3713	Salmon - VY LT						3802	Antique Mauve - VY DK					
3716	Dusty Rose - VY LT						3803	Mauve - DK					
3721	Shell Pink - DK						3804	Cyclamen Pink - DK					
3722	Shell Pink - MED						3805	Cyclamen Pink					
3726	Antique Mauve - DK						3806	Cyclamen Pink - LT					
3727	Antique Mauve - LT						3807	Cornflower Blue					
3731	Dusty Rose - VY DK						3808	Turquoise - ULT VY DK					
3733	Dusty Rose						3809	Turquoise - VY DK					
3740	Antique Violet - DK						3810	Turquoise - DK					
3743	Antique Violet - VY LT						3811	Turquoise - VY LT					
3746	Blue Violet - DK						3812	Seagreen - VY DK					
3747	Blue Violet - VY LT						3813	Blue Green - LT					
3750	Antique Blue - VY DK						3814	Aquamarine					
3752	Antique Blue - VY LT						3815	Celadon Green - DK					
3753	Antique Blue - ULT VY LT						3816	Celadon Green					
3755	Baby Blue						3817	Celadon Green - LT					
3756	Baby Blue - LT						3818	Emerald Green - ULT VY D					

3819 - 3866

No.	Name	Colour	SQ	RND	AB SQ	AB RND	No.	Name	Colour	SQ	RND	AB SQ	AB RND
3819	Moss Green - LT						3856	Mahogany - ULT VY LT					
3820	Straw - DK						3857	Rosewood - DK					
3821	Straw						3858	Rosewood - MED					
3822	Straw - LT						3859	Rosewood - LT					
3823	Yellow - ULT PALE						3860	Cocoa					
3824	Apricot - LT						3861	Cocoa - LT					
3825	Pumpkin - PALE						3862	Mocha Beige - DK					
3826	Golden Brown						3863	Mocha Beige - MED					
3827	Golden Brown - PALE						3864	Mocha Beige - LT					
3828	Hazelnut Brown						3865	Winter White					
3829	Old Gold - VY DK						3866	Mocha Brown - ULT VY LT					
3830	Terra Cotta							The Following is only available in the US at this time.					
3831	Raspberry - DK												
3832	Raspberry - MED												
3833	Raspberry - LT						3880	Shell Pink - MED VY DK					
3834	Grape - DK						3881	Avocado Green - PALE					
3835	Grape - MED						3882	Cocoa - MED LT					
3836	Grape - LT						3883	Copper - MED LT					
3837	Lavender - ULT DK						3884	Pewter - MED LT					
3838	Lavender Blue - DK						3885	Blue - MED VY DK					
3839	Lavender Blue - MED						3886	Plum - VY DK					
3840	Lavender Blue - LT						3887	Lavender - ULT VY DK					
3841	Baby Blue - PALE						3888	Antique Violet - MED DK					
3842	Wedgewood - DK						3889	Lemon - MED LT					
3843	Electric Blue						3890	Turquoise - VY LT BRIGHT					
3844	Bright Turquoise - DK						3891	Turquoise - VY DK BRIGHT					
3845	Bright Turquoise - MED						3892	Orange Spice - MED LT					
3846	Bright Turquoise - LT						3893	Mocha Beige - VY LT					
3847	Teal Green - DK						3894	Parrot Green - VY LT					
3848	Teal Green - MED						3895	Beaver Gray - MED DK					
3849	Teal Green - LT						5200	Snow White					
3850	Bright Green - DK												
3851	Bright Green - LT												
3852	Straw - VY DK												
3853	Autumn Gold - DK												
3854	Autumn Gold - MED												
3855	Autumn Gold - LT												

Diamond Painting Timesheet

Project	Date	Time Started	Time Ended	Total Time
	/ /	:	:	:
	/ /	:	:	:
	/ /	:	:	:
	/ /	:	:	:
	/ /	:	:	:
	/ /	:	:	:
	/ /	:	:	:
	/ /	:	:	:
	/ /	:	:	:
	/ /	:	:	:
	/ /	:	:	:
	/ /	:	:	:
	/ /	:	:	:
	/ /	:	:	:
	/ /	:	:	:
	/ /	:	:	:
	/ /	:	:	:
	/ /	:	:	:
	/ /	:	:	:
	/ /	:	:	:
	/ /	:	:	:
	/ /	:	:	:
	/ /	:	:	:
	/ /	:	:	:

Diamond Painting Timesheet

Project	Date	Time Started	Time Ended	Total Time
	/ /	:	:	:
	/ /	:	:	:
	/ /	:	:	:
	/ /	:	:	:
	/ /	:	:	:
	/ /	:	:	:
	/ /	:	:	:
	/ /	:	:	:
	/ /	:	:	:
	/ /	:	:	:
	/ /	:	:	:
	/ /	:	:	:
	/ /	:	:	:
	/ /	:	:	:
	/ /	:	:	:
	/ /	:	:	:
	/ /	:	:	:
	/ /	:	:	:
	/ /	:	:	:
	/ /	:	:	:
	/ /	:	:	:
	/ /	:	:	:
	/ /	:	:	:

Diamond Painting Log Book

Project/Kit/Painting name: _____

Purchased from: _____   Gifted by: _____

Canvas size: _____

Date started: _____   Diamond type: ☐ ○

Date finished: _____   Regular: ☐ ○

                                    Aurora Borealis: ☐ ○

Total Drills: _____   Notes: _____

Finished piece: Sold ○   Kept ○   Gifted ○   Framed: yes/no

Notes from sale: _____

If gifted, to whom? _____

Difficulty level: Easy ○   Moderate ○   Difficult ○

Overall project rating: ☆ ☆ ☆ ☆ ☆

Notes:

_____

_____

_____

Photo/Notes

Diamond Painting Log Book

Project/Kit/Painting name: _____

Purchased from: _____   Gifted by: _____

Canvas size: _____

Date started: _____

Diamond type: ☐ ○

Regular: ☐ ○

Date finished: _____

Aurora Borealis: ☐ ○

Total Drills: _____   Notes: _____

Finished piece: Sold ○   Kept ○   Gifted ○   Framed: yes/no

Notes from sale: _____

If gifted, to whom? _____

Difficulty level: Easy ○   Moderate ○   Difficult ○

Overall project rating: ☆ ☆ ☆ ☆ ☆

Notes:

_____

_____

_____

Photo/Notes

Diamond Painting Log Book

Project/Kit/Painting name: _____

Purchased from: _____   Gifted by: _____

Canvas size: _____

Date started: _____   Diamond type: ☐ ○

Date finished: _____   Regular: ☐ ○

Aurora Borealis: ☐ ○

Total Drills: _____   Notes: _____

Finished piece: Sold ○   Kept ○   Gifted ○   Framed: yes/no

Notes from sale: _____

If gifted, to whom? _____

Difficulty level: Easy ○   Moderate ○   Difficult ○

Overall project rating: ☆ ☆ ☆ ☆ ☆

Notes:

_____

_____

_____

Photo/Notes

Diamond Painting Log Book

Project/Kit/Painting name: _____

Purchased from: _____ Gifted by: _____

Canvas size: _____

Diamond type: ☐ ○

Date started: _____

Regular: ☐ ○

Date finished: _____

Aurora Borealis: ☐ ○

Total Drills: _____ Notes: _____

Finished piece: Sold ○   Kept ○   Gifted ○   Framed: yes/no

Notes from sale: _____

If gifted, to whom? _____

Difficulty level: Easy ○   Moderate ○   Difficult ○

Overall project rating: ☆ ☆ ☆ ☆ ☆

Notes:

_____
_____
_____

Photo/Notes

Diamond Painting Log Book

Project/Kit/Painting name: _____

Purchased from: _____   Gifted by: _____

Canvas size: _____

Date started: _____   Diamond type: ☐ ○

Date finished: _____   Regular: ☐ ○

                                  Aurora Borealis: ☐ ○

Total Drills: _____   Notes: _____

Finished piece: Sold ○   Kept ○   Gifted ○   Framed: yes/no

Notes from sale: _____

If gifted, to whom? _____

Difficulty level: Easy ○   Moderate ○   Difficult ○

Overall project rating: ☆ ☆ ☆ ☆ ☆

Notes:

_____

_____

_____

Photo/Notes

Diamond Painting Log Book

Project/Kit/Painting name: _____

Purchased from: _____   Gifted by: _____

Canvas size: _____

Date started: _____   Diamond type: ☐ ○

Date finished: _____   Regular: ☐ ○

Aurora Borealis: ☐ ○

Total Drills: _____   Notes: _____

Finished piece: Sold ○   Kept ○   Gifted ○   Framed: yes/no

Notes from sale: _____

If gifted, to whom? _____

Difficulty level: Easy ○   Moderate ○   Difficult ○

Overall project rating: ☆ ☆ ☆ ☆ ☆

Notes:

_____
_____
_____

Photo/Notes

Diamond Painting Log Book

Project/Kit/Painting name: _____

Purchased from: _____ Gifted by: _____

Canvas size: _____

Date started: _____ Diamond type: ☐ ○

Date finished: _____ Regular: ☐ ○

Aurora Borealis: ☐ ○

Total Drills: _____ Notes: _____

Finished piece: Sold ○   Kept ○   Gifted ○   Framed: yes/no

Notes from sale: _____

If gifted, to whom? _____

Difficulty level: Easy ○   Moderate ○   Difficult ○

Overall project rating: ☆ ☆ ☆ ☆ ☆

Notes:

_____

_____

_____

Photo/Notes

Diamond Painting Log Book

Project/Kit/Painting name: _____

Purchased from: _____ Gifted by: _____

Canvas size: _____

Diamond type: ☐ ○

Date started: _____

Regular: ☐ ○

Date finished: _____

Aurora Borealis: ☐ ○

Total Drills: _____ Notes: _____

Finished piece: Sold ○   Kept ○   Gifted ○   Framed: yes/no

Notes from sale: _____

If gifted, to whom? _____

Difficulty level: Easy ○   Moderate ○   Difficult ○

Overall project rating: ☆ ☆ ☆ ☆ ☆

Notes:

_____

_____

_____

Photo/Notes

Diamond Painting Log Book

Project/Kit/Painting name: _____

Purchased from: _____   Gifted by: _____

Canvas size: _____

Date started: _____   Diamond type: ☐ ○

Regular: ☐ ○

Date finished: _____   Aurora Borealis: ☐ ○

Total Drills: _____   Notes: _____

Finished piece: Sold ○   Kept ○   Gifted ○   Framed: yes/no

Notes from sale: _____

If gifted, to whom? _____

Difficulty level: Easy ○   Moderate ○   Difficult ○

Overall project rating: ☆ ☆ ☆ ☆ ☆

Notes:

_____

_____

_____

Photo/Notes

Diamond Painting Log Book

Project/Kit/Painting name: _____

Purchased from: _____   Gifted by: _____

Canvas size: _____

Date started: _____   Diamond type: ☐ ◯

Date finished: _____   Regular: ☐ ◯

Aurora Borealis: ☐ ◯

Total Drills: _____   Notes: _____

Finished piece: Sold ◯   Kept ◯   Gifted ◯   Framed: yes/no

Notes from sale: _____

If gifted, to whom? _____

Difficulty level: Easy ◯   Moderate ◯   Difficult ◯

Overall project rating: ☆ ☆ ☆ ☆ ☆

Notes:

_____

_____

_____

Photo/Notes

Diamond Painting Log Book

Project/Kit/Painting name: _____

Purchased from: _____   Gifted by: _____

Canvas size: _____

Date started: _____   Diamond type: ☐ ○

Date finished: _____   Regular: ☐ ○

                                     Aurora Borealis: ☐ ○

Total Drills: _____   Notes: _____

Finished piece: Sold ○   Kept ○   Gifted ○   Framed: yes/no

Notes from sale: _____

If gifted, to whom? _____

Difficulty level: Easy ○   Moderate ○   Difficult ○

Overall project rating: ☆ ☆ ☆ ☆ ☆

Notes:

_____

_____

_____

Photo/Notes

Diamond Painting Log Book

Project/Kit/Painting name: _____

Purchased from: _____   Gifted by: _____

Canvas size: _____

Date started: _____   Diamond type: ☐ ○

Date finished: _____   Regular: ☐ ○

Aurora Borealis: ☐ ○

Total Drills: _____   Notes: _____

Finished piece: Sold ○   Kept ○   Gifted ○   Framed: yes/no

Notes from sale: _____

If gifted, to whom? _____

Difficulty level: Easy ○   Moderate ○   Difficult ○

Overall project rating: ☆ ☆ ☆ ☆ ☆

Notes:

_____

_____

_____

Photo/Notes

Diamond Painting Log Book

Project/Kit/Painting name: _____

Purchased from: _____ Gifted by: _____

Painting size: _____

Date started: _____   Diamond type: ☐ ○

Date finished: _____   Regular: ☐ ○

                                  Aurora Borealis: ☐ ○

Total Drills: _____   Notes: _____

Finished piece: Sold ○   Kept ○   Gifted ○   Framed: yes/no

Notes from sale: _____

If gifted, to whom? _____

Difficulty level: Easy ○   Moderate ○   Difficult ○

Overall project rating: ☆ ☆ ☆ ☆ ☆

Notes:

_____

_____

_____

Photo/Notes

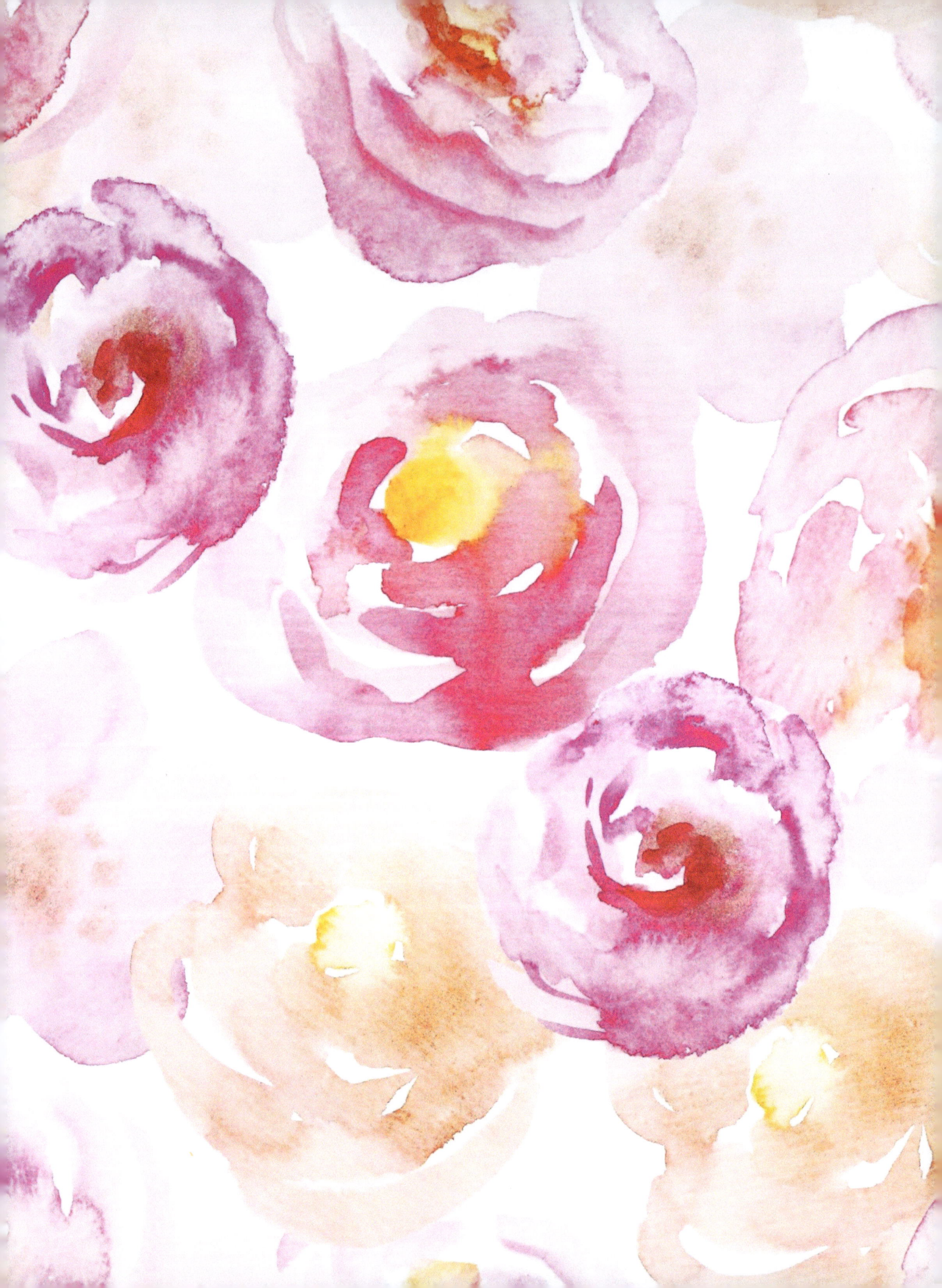

A little gift

- Cut out both shapes.

- To assemble, fold along the dashed lines, with the printed lines on the inside of the fold.

- Glue the sides together along the small flaps, and then glue small hexagon for the top last.

- Glue the top and bottom together.

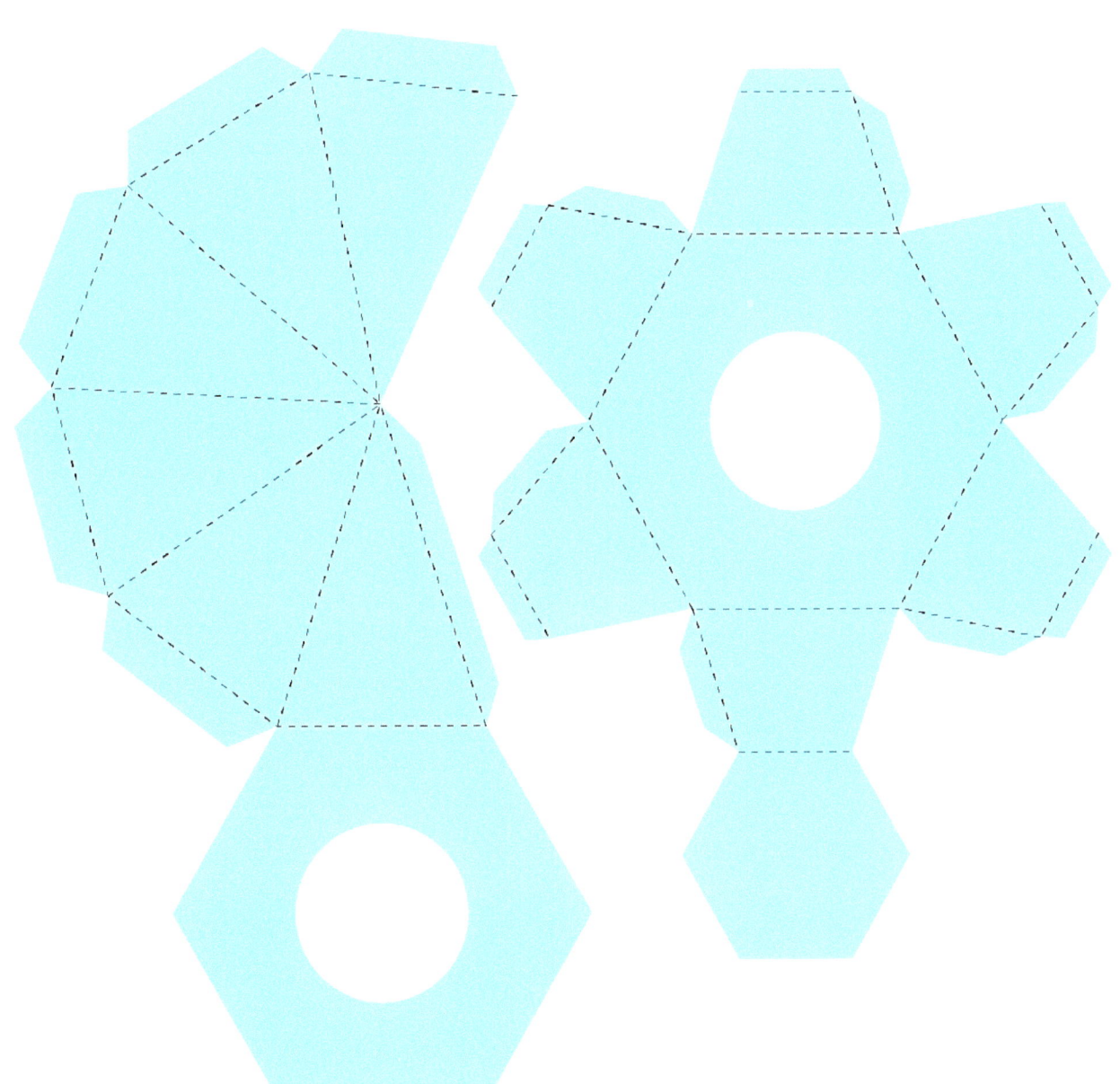

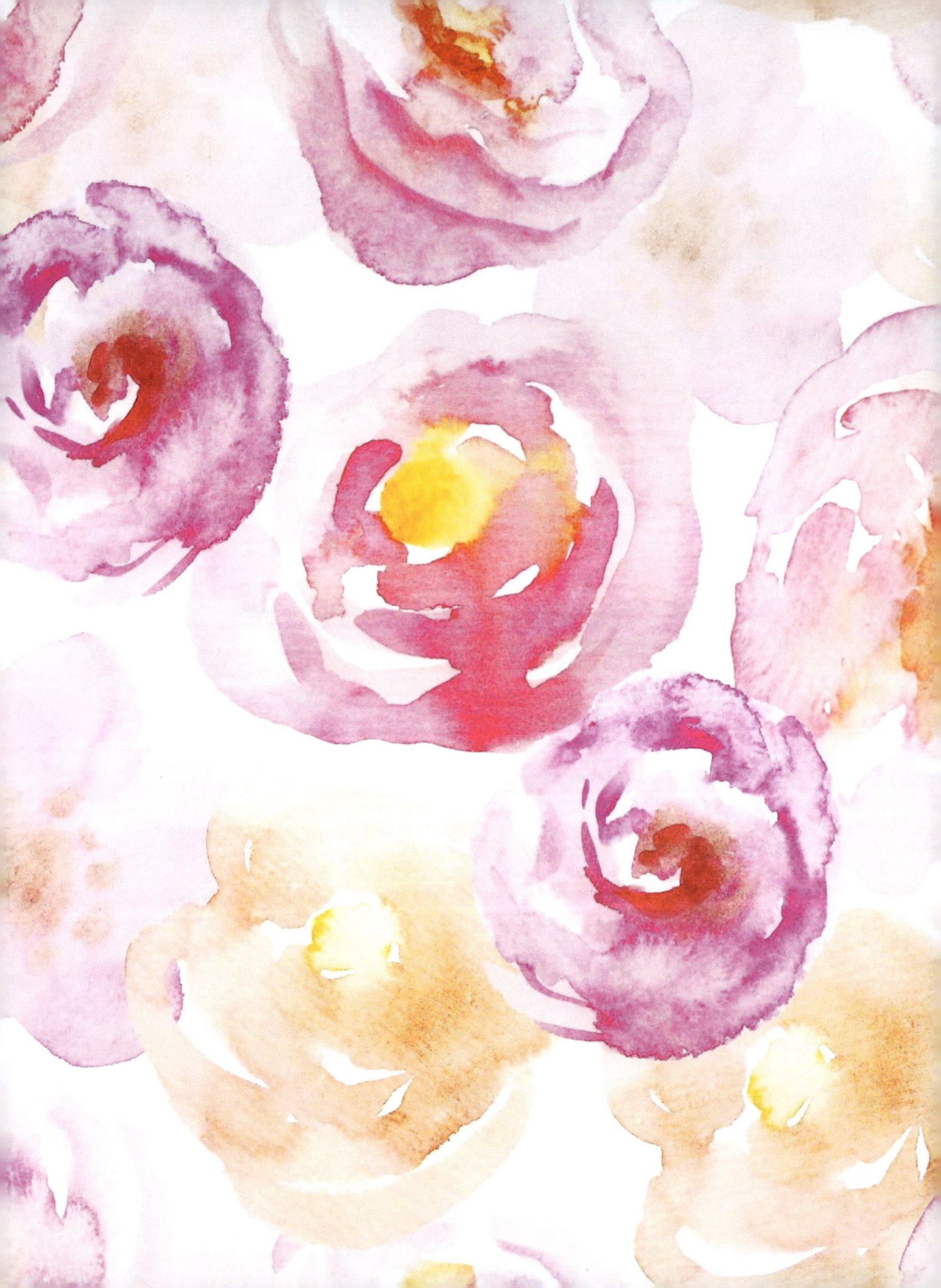